Thomas Jefferson

Thomas Jefferson

Don Nardo

AMERICA'S

3RD

PRESIDENT

Children's Press®
A Division of Scholastic Inc.
New York / Toronto / London / Auckland / Sydney
Mexico City / New Delhi / Hong Kong
Danbury, Connecticut

Library of Congress Cataloging-in-Publication Data

Nardo, Don, 1947-
    Thomas Jefferson / by Don Nardo.
      p. cm.—(Encyclopedia of presidents)
    Summary: Discusses the childhood, family life, political career, two terms
as President, and accomplishments of Thomas Jefferson.
Includes bibliographical references and index.
 ISBN 0-516-22768-8
  1. Jefferson, Thomas, 1743-1826—Juvenile literature. 2. Presidents—United
States—Biography—Juvenile literature. [1. Jefferson, Thomas, 1743-1826.
2. Presidents.] I. Title. II. Series.
E332.79 .N37 2003
973.4'6'092—dc21   2002008272

Contents

Most Versatile President ——————

The period in which the British colonies of North America became the United States was rich in new ideas and brave deeds. Many gifted and energetic individuals contributed to the intellectual, political, and military actions that made the colonies independent and established them as a nation. One of the most extraordinary of all was a tall, shy, brilliant man named Thomas Jefferson.

Jefferson was the most versatile and talented of the Founding Fathers. The roles he played include patriot, politician, statesman, diplomat, writer, scientist, inventor, and architect. So great was his contribution to his country and to humanity in general that one admirer remarked, "Taken as a whole, history presents nothing so grand, so beautiful . . . in all the great points as the life and character of Thomas Jefferson."

Exploring Hidden Valleys ——————————

That life began on April 13, 1743. At Shadwell, a 400-acre (162-hectare) planta-tion on the banks of the Rivanna River in Britain's colony of Virginia, Peter and Jane Randolph Jefferson had a son, whom they named Thomas. He was the old-est of ten children. Two died in infancy, leaving two sons and six daughters.

A surveyor and a lieutenant colonel in the Virginia militia, Peter Jefferson had married Jane Randolph, a member of one of the wealthiest and most power-ful families in the region. Thomas Jefferson grew up as part of a local *aristocracy*, or privileged class. He would receive a demanding education, preparing him to be a landowner and a lawyer.

Peter Jefferson was from a less prominent family and had received little formal education. Yet the plants, animals, and rolling hills near Shadwell fasci-nated him. He passed his wonder and curiosity about nature on to young Thomas, encouraging the boy to carry notebooks with him at all times and to jot down everything he found interesting. Thomas recorded his observations in unusual detail. As a child, he filled many notebooks with information on the sizes, colors, habits, and activities of the animals and insects he saw. The boy and his father sometimes rode their horses all day, exploring new trails and small hidden val-leys. Hundreds of square miles of wilderness stretched westward from their home into the Blue Ridge Mountains.

Some of what is known about Jefferson's relatives comes from his autobiography, which he began writing in 1821 when he was 77 years old. In this excerpt, he briefly mentions his mother:

> My father's education had been quite neglected; but being of a strong mind, sound judgment and eager after information, he read much and improved himself. . . . He died . . . [in 1757], leaving my mother a widow who lived till 1776, with 6 daughters & 2 sons, myself the elder. To my younger brother he left the estate on James River called Snowdon. . . . To myself [he left] the lands on which I was born & live.

★ ★ ☆

That Special Hilltop

Thomas also took jaunts into the countryside with friends to enjoy hunting, fishing, and exploring. He went with his cousin, Thomas Mann Randolph, or with neighbors John Page or Dabney Carr. According to a family story, Jefferson and Carr found a very special place one day. After traveling through virgin forest, they climbed a hill. From the top they could see lushly forested mountaintops that seemed to stretch to the horizon, their colors fading from green to blue to pale violet.

The boys gazed at this sight for a long moment. Then Carr said that this was where he wanted to be buried when he died. To Jefferson this special hilltop was suitable for the living as well as the dead. He told Carr that this was where he would build his home someday.

This early view looks from the hilltop on which Jefferson built his estate toward Charlottesville, Virginia. Shadwell, his birth-place, was nearby.

Jefferson kept both promises. In 1770, when he was in his late twenties, he began building the house he called Monticello on that very spot. Meanwhile, Dabney Carr had married Jefferson's youngest sister, Martha. In 1773, at the age of 29, Dabney Carr died. Remembering their boyhood conversation, Jefferson buried Carr on the same hilltop. Beside the grave he placed a marker stone with these words: "Dabney Carr: To his virtue, good sense, learning, and friendship, this stone is dedicated by Thomas Jefferson, who of all men living loved him most."

Jefferson also took in and cared for Martha and her six children. They lived with him at Monticello for many years. He treated young Peter Carr like a son.

An Education Befitting an Aristocrat ———

Jefferson received his early education close to home. After learning to read and write, he studied Latin and Greek with a local minister. Many boys studied these ancient languages, but Jefferson was one of the few who came to love them. He read and admired poetry and history written in Latin and Greek for the rest of his life. Years later, he wrote:

> To read the Latin and Greek authors in their original is a sublime
>
> luxury. I thank on my knees him who directed my early education for

having put into my possession this rich source of delight; and I would

not exchange it for anything which I could have then acquired, and

have not since acquired.

Other sons of Virginia landowners received the same kind of education as

Jefferson. As members of a privileged class, they could expect to go on to college

and then become gentlemen planters. They would supervise their plantations and

govern their local communities. Perhaps they would become members of the

House of Burgesses, the colony's legislature, which enacted local laws affecting

Virginia.

Most members of Virginia's landed class saw themselves as superior to

the poor farmers, merchants, and laborers, not to mention the slaves brought from

Africa who did much of the hard labor on the plantations. Although Jefferson

grew up in this privileged class, even as a teenager he did not share that sense of

superiority. He came to believe that judging people by who their families were

and how rich they were was useless—many planters were neither good nor tal-

ented. He wrote that there is a different "natural" aristocracy based on virtue and

talents—these are what qualify a person to teach or govern others.

Still, young Jefferson was tempted by the pleasures of wealthy young

men. Many gave up their studies early and spent their days playing cards, fox-hunting, and racing horses. Without a father to govern him, the teenaged Jefferson might have taken up such an idle life. He confessed many years later to a relative:

> When I recollect that at fourteen years of age the whole care and
> direction of myself was thrown on myself entirely . . . and recollect the
> various sorts of bad company with which I associated from time to
> time, I am astonished that I did not . . . become as worthless to society
> as they were. . . . Many a time I have asked myself . . . which of these
> kinds of reputation should I prefer, that of a horse-jockey . . . or the
> honest advocate of my country's rights?

Like other young men in Virginia's aristocracy, Jefferson enjoyed racing fast horses.

Higher Learning

In 1760, just before turning 17, Jefferson began his studies at the College of William and Mary. It had been established only 67 years earlier in Williamsburg, the colonial capital, and named for the king and queen of England at that time.

Jefferson had already attained most of his adult features. He was tall and lean, with large hands and feet. His hair was reddish, his skin ruddy and freckled, his eyes light brown, and his nose angular and noble-looking. He was an eager student and learned quickly. Mathematics professor William Small recognized Jefferson's brilliant mind. The two spent many hours outside of class discussing science and *philosophy*, the study of ideas and the meaning of life.

Professor Small also introduced Jefferson to a prominent lawyer, George Wythe. In 1762, Jefferson finished his college studies and decided to study law. For the next five years, he studied with Wythe, who became a close friend. In addition to studying, Jefferson sat with Wythe in court, copied out documents, did research, and ran errands.

Because Williamsburg was also the colonial capital, Jefferson was soon following the government and politics of the colony. The royal governor, appointed by the British king, lived in Williamsburg. The House of Burgesses, made up of Viriginians who helped make laws for the colony, met there. The speaker of the house was Peyton Randolph, a relative of Jefferson on his mother's side.

The Wren Building at the College of William and Mary (center) was already 60 years old when Thomas Jefferson enrolled at the college.

The Enlightenment

One young lawyer who befriended Jefferson in Williamsburg was Patrick Henry.

Only seven years older than Jefferson, Henry was a member of the House of

Burgesses, and was a student of philosophy and politics. Like many young men

of the time, Henry was fascinated by the ideas of thinkers in Europe (mainly in

France and Britain) who believed that reason should guide people's actions and

their governments. These writers argued for basic human rights, including free-

dom of thought, speech, and religion. We call their movement the Enlightenment.

The Enlightenment thinker who influenced Henry and other American patriots the most was Englishman John Locke, who lived from 1632 to 1704. Locke argued that people have natural human rights and that societies ruled by kings usually deny people many of these rights. People have a right to agree to their government, he said, and if a ruler ignores that right, they are justified in removing their ruler and forming a new government.

Thomas Jefferson was deeply impressed by the ideas of Locke and other Enlightenment writers. When the British king began restricting the rights of the colonists, Jefferson followed Locke's reasoning to explain the need for throwing off the British government and establishing a new government. Before long, Locke's words would echo in the Declaration of Independence. The author of that famous declaration was Thomas Jefferson.

Locke on Natural Rights

In his *Second Treatise of Government*, published in 1690, John Locke wrote:

The state of nature has a law of nature to govern it . . . and reason, which is that law, teaches all mankind . . . that, being equal and independent, no one ought to harm another in his life, health, liberty or possession. . . . And that all men may be restrained from invading others' rights and from doing hurt to one another, and the law of nature be observed, which wills the peace and preservation of all mankind, the execution of the law of nature is . . . put into every man's hands.

☆☆☆

Chapter 2

Conflict with Great Britain —————

As a young law student in the Virginia capital, Thomas Jefferson found himself drawn into the debates and conflicts that swept through the American colonies in the late 1760s. He soon discovered he had a great talent for political and legal affairs. In addition, he knew many of the leading Virginians of his day, including Peyton Randolph, Patrick Henry, and George Wythe. All these men watched as the relationship between Britain and its colonies got steadily worse. What should the colonists do? Could they persuade the British to treat them more fairly? What actions could they take?

In 1765, the British imposed the Stamp Act, which placed *duties*, or taxes, on paper used for legal and business documents, newspapers, pamphlets, playing cards, and other products. Colonists of all walks of life felt the Stamp Act was unfair, and they protested. Angry crowds threatened tax collectors and other British officials. In some cases they even attacked the officials or burned down their houses.

The colonial legislatures were also defiant. In the House of Burgesses, Patrick Henry made a fiery speech against the Stamp Act. When one of the spectators accused Henry of *treason*, or taking sides against his own country, he daringly replied, "If this be treason, make the most of it!" As Jefferson later wrote, Henry helped set the ball of revolution in motion.

In 1767, Jefferson took and passed the examination which qualified him to practice law. He left Williamsburg and began his practice where he grew up, in Albemarle County. The next year, his neighbors chose him to represent his home region in the House of Burgesses.

Abuses of One Are Abuses of All —————

Jefferson took his seat in the House of Burgesses at a dramatic time. He joined with other members in drafting a formal protest to *Parliament*, Britain's legislature. Britain had repealed the Stamp Act, but then imposed new taxes on the colonies. The Virginians' protest argued that Parliament should not dictate local colonial policies, especially relating to taxes. Virginia's governor, Lord Botetourt,

The fiery Patrick Henry later roused the Virginia legislature to fight for independence. In his most famous speech, he shouted, "Give me liberty or give me death!"

Lord Botetourt, the royal governor who closed down the House of Burgesses, was also a generous contributor to the College of William and Mary, where this statue of him stands today.

who was appointed by the king, answered the protest by *dissolving*, or closing down, the House of Burgesses. The members continued to meet in secret and began a campaign to end the purchase of any goods taxed by Parliament.

The Burgesses were soon allowed to meet publicly again. But in 1773, a second dispute arose. This time it concerned a court ruling in Rhode Island that people accused of a crime in the colonies could be taken away to England for trial, where it would be almost impossible for them to defend themselves. The

Burgesses wrote a protest, and Lord Dunmore, the new British governor, dissolved the session. Once again, its members continued to meet privately.

Similar events were taking place in Massachusetts and other colonies. Also during 1773, patriots in Boston boarded a British merchant ship and emptied chests of taxed tea into the harbor. Many colonists were beginning to see that British abuses against one colony amounted to an abuse against all the colonies. The colonies set up committees of correspondence whose job it was to stay in constant touch and help coordinate their plans. One of the first recommendations was that the colonies call a general meeting at which delegates from all the colonies could discuss the situation in person and take any necessary action. Jefferson recalled these events years later in his autobiography:

> We were all sensible that the most urgent of all measures was that of coming to an understanding with all the other colonies, to consider the British claims as a common cause to all, and to produce a unity of action; and, for this purpose, that committees of correspondence in each colony would be the best instrument of intercommunication: and that their first measure would probably be to propose a meeting of deputies from every colony, at some central place, who should be charged with the direction of measures which should be taken by all.

A New Home and Marriage —————————

These activities occupied only part of Jefferson's time during these years. He spent many hours each week attending to his law practice. He also began a project he had long dreamed about—building a house on that special hilltop near Shadwell. Having a natural gift for architecture, he began designing the project in 1767. The following year, he hired workers to clear rocks, trees, and brush from the summit. Then in 1769, Jefferson oversaw the digging of the house's foundations. He also settled on a name. The estate would be called Monticello, Italian for "little mountain."

It was lucky Jefferson began the house when he did. In November of 1770, he was forced to move into Monticello long before it was finished after a terrible fire destroyed his family home at Shadwell. Countless memories went up in smoke, but Jefferson was particularly upset about the loss of his large collection of books and papers. In a letter to his friend, John Page, he complained:

> On a reasonable estimate, I calculate the cost of the books to have been 200 sterling [i.e., 200 English pounds, a large sum at the time]. Would to God it had been [only] money; then had it never cost me a sigh! To make the loss more sensible, it fell principally on my books of common law, of which I have but one left, at the time lent out. Of papers too, of

every kind I am utterly destitute. All of those, whether public or private,

of business or amusement, have perished in the flames.

Jefferson went to live in the only finished wing at Monticello, a single

room 18 feet (5.5 meters) on a side. Workmen came and went, slowly building

more of the house. About this time, he met Martha Wayles Skelton, a 23 year-

old widow from the Williamsburg area. After a courtship of little more than a

The South Pavilion at Monticello was the first part of the estate to be built. Jefferson brought his wife Martha to this small "cottage" after their wedding.

year, they were married on New Year's Day in 1772. Many years later, their daughter, Martha, recalled that the happy couple approached Monticello during a snowstorm. "They were finally obliged to quit the carriage and proceed on horseback. . . . [They made] their way through a mountain track rather than a road, in which the snow lay from eighteen inches to two feet deep. . . . They arrived at night, the fires all out and the servants retired to their own houses for the night."

Jefferson Addresses the King

Larger events continued to swirl around Jefferson. Responding to continued unrest in the colonies, in 1774 Parliament passed what the colonists called the Intolerable Acts. These acts closed Boston Harbor to all shipping except food and medical supplies, and authorized British troops to take over unused public buildings for lodgings.

Angry at these measures, the colonies agreed to send representatives to Philadelphia in September 1774 to decide how to respond. This gathering was known as the First Continental Congress. Jefferson wrote a long essay called *A Summary View of the Rights of British America* to help prepare the Virginia delegates for the Congress. In it, he addressed King George III directly, calling on the British ruler and his government to be reasonable:

Kings are the servants, not the proprietors [owners] of the people.
Open your breast, Sire, to liberal and expanded thought. Let not the
name of George the Third be a blot in the page of history. . . . It
behoves [is proper for] you, therefore, to think and to act for yourself
and your people. The great principles of right and wrong are legible
to every reader; to pursue them requires not the aid of many
counsellors. The whole art of government consists in the art of being
honest. Only aim to do your duty, and mankind will give you credit
where you fail. No longer persevere [continue] in sacrificing the
rights of one part of the empire to the inordinate [unreasonable]
desires of another; but deal out to all, equal and impartial right. . . .
We are willing on our part, to sacrifice every thing which reason can
ask to the restoration of that tranquility [state of peace] for which all
must wish.

Among the grievances Jefferson listed in his *Summary View* was an objection to the king's sending foreign-born British troops to American soil:

His Majesty has, from time to time, sent among us large bodies of
armed forces, not made up of the people here, nor raised by the
authority of our laws. Did his Majesty possess such a right as this, it

might swallow up all our other rights. . . . His Majesty has no right to land a single armed man on our shores; and those whom he sends here are liable to our laws.

Time for Radical Action

The king and Parliament did not act reasonably, as Jefferson and his fellow patriots had hoped. Tensions continued to mount. In April 1775, a group of British troops marched on the villages of Concord and Lexington, west of Boston, to seize armaments and ammunition. Local colonial militiamen responded, and the two sides fought the first major skirmishes of the Revolutionary War. Men on both sides were killed and wounded.

Colonial leaders now feared that the only way to resolve their differences with Britain might be to separate from that nation. Jefferson and other moderates still hoped that the two parties might come to terms. Then King George declared that the colonies were in open rebellion and began preparing to crush them. This convinced even the moderates that radical action was necessary. At the Second Continental Congress, which met in the spring of 1776, Virginia's Richard Henry Lee introduced a daring resolution. As Jefferson later recalled, it declared that the colonies "are, and of right ought to be, free and independent states, [and] that they are absolved from all allegiance to the British crown."

On June 11, Congress appointed a committee to draft a document announcing and justifying the colonies' independence. It included Jefferson, John Adams of Massachusetts, Robert R. Livingston of New York, Benjamin Franklin of Pennsylvania, and Roger Sherman of Connecticut. The five men met briefly and discussed the general form of the document. Recognizing Jefferson's talents as a writer, Franklin and the others asked Jefferson to prepare the first draft.

A Document for the Ages

Jefferson wrote the initial draft of the Declaration of Independence between June 12 and 28, 1776. The work took place in a parlor on the second floor of a rented house on the corner of Seventh and Market Streets in Philadelphia. One of Jefferson's aims was to present to the world a moral argument for the rightness of the colonies' split with Britain. The main body of the document consists of a list of charges of abuse by Britain. One charge says that the king had closed down local legislatures "repeatedly and continually for opposing . . . his invasions on the rights of the people." Another claims, "He has kept among us in times of peace standing armies and ships of war without the consent of our legislatures."

A sketch of the house in Philadelphia where Jefferson wrote the first draft of the Declaration of Independence. The building still stands and has been restored.

Jefferson's other goal was to state the political philosophy of the new nation. For this he drew freely on the ideals of John Locke and other Enlightenment writers. In the second paragraph of the draft, Jefferson wrote, "We hold these truths to be sacred and undeniable, that all men are created equal and independent." (Jefferson later changed "sacred and undeniable" to "self-evident.") To secure people's civil rights, he continued, "governments are insti-

tuted among men, deriving their just powers from the consent of the governed."
Further, if a government denies its citizens their rights, they are justified in abolishing that government and creating a new and fairer one.

Jefferson asked Franklin and Adams to review his draft, and they suggested minor revisions. He submitted it to the full committee, which suggested other small changes. Then on June 28, the committee submitted the completed version to Congress for debate and approval.

The committee presents the Declaration of Independence to the Congress. Jefferson is the tallest of the group, John Adams is at the left, and Benjamin Franklin stands next to Jefferson on the right.

It was clear that Jefferson had created more than a simple justification for declaring independence. The work is a document for the ages—a timeless statement of human dignity and human rights. It became the chief statement of the creed of the United States, and it inspired others in many parts of the world to struggle for governments that protect human dignity and human rights.

Chapter 3

Working for Virginia ——————

After the Continental Congress issued the Declaration of Independence, Thomas Jefferson went back to Monticello, hoping to devote his attention to his family, his landholdings, and his law practice. He still hoped that the king and Parliament might grant the colonies independence peacefully, but there were many signs that the war would only grow larger.

One interest Jefferson returned to was the affairs of his beloved Virginia. Only a few weeks before he left for the Second Continental Congress, he had finished a draft of a new constitution for the state. When he returned, Jefferson took his place as a member in the House of Delegates, part of the newly organized Virginia legislature. There he continued to work for major reforms in law and government.

For generations, a few wealthy families had controlled most of the productive lands in Virginia. One of the laws that helped them keep control involved inheritance. When a plantation owner died, his oldest son automatically inherited the estate. As a result, large estates were almost never broken up into smaller plots, so productive land rarely was available to poorer farmers. Jefferson helped push through new measures that changed the inheritance laws and opened up vast amounts of land to Virginia's small farmers. He believed that "natural aristocrats," small farmers who were intelligent and energetic, would become the backbone of the new republic.

Jefferson also introduced legislation designed to separate the affairs of the state from the affairs of the church. In Virginia, the government supported the Anglican Church (part of the Church of England). It set aside money to pay Anglican ministers and to care for Anglican churches and other properties. But in the 1700s, fewer and fewer of the poor ever went to an Anglican church. Some went to Methodist or Baptist meetinghouses. Some established Presbyterian and other churches without any state support. Many others attended no church at all. There were similar situations in the other colonies.

Jefferson believed that the state-supported church had too much power in Virginia, as well as in other states. He believed it was unfair that people's taxes paid for a church that most of them never went to. Although he believed in God,

The capitol in Williamsburg where the House of Burgesses met before independence and the House of Delegates met after independence. In 1779, when Jefferson was governor, the state capital was moved from Williamsburg to Richmond.

he thought that a state should not impose a particular religion on individuals. Religion should be a private matter rather than a public one, he said. Furthermore, no person should be judged by which church he or she attends, nor should someone be judged for choosing not to attend any church. There should be, therefore, both freedom *of* religion and freedom *from* religion. He wrote in 1785:

> It does me no injury for my neighbor to say there are twenty gods, or
> no god. Millions of innocent men, women, and children, since the
> introduction of Christianity, have been burned, tortured, fined,
> imprisoned; yet we have not advanced one inch toward uniformity [of
> belief]. . . . Let us reflect that [the earth has] . . . a thousand different
> religions. That ours is only one of a thousand. . . . We cannot [convert
> the others to our beliefs] by force. Reason and persuasion are the only
> practicable instruments. . . . The way to silence religious disputes is to
> take no notice of them.

In 1779, Jefferson proposed a bill for religious freedom in Virginia's legislature. Many of the other legislators were shocked by the idea. Churches supported by the government existed in nearly every country in Europe and in most of the colonies. The idea of separating church and state seemed too radical, and Jefferson's bill did not pass. Only seven years later, however, under the direction of Jefferson's close friend and follower, James Madison, the bill was enacted. Jefferson viewed this as one of his most important accomplishments. The Virginia bill later became the model for similar bills in other states and in the country as a whole.

A third issue Jefferson fought for was public education. In his time, schools were run by private individuals and corporations. Any student who wanted to attend a school had to pay tuition—a fee to cover the cost of teaching. Students older than about twelve years old often had to study in a town far from their homes, so they also had to pay room and board—fees for a place to sleep and for food. As a legislator, Jefferson called for education to be provided by local governments for all children, rich and poor alike. Again, the legislature thought the idea was too radical—and far too expensive. In later years, however, people came to see the wisdom of public schools. Within a hundred years, most towns and cities in nearly every state provided free public schools.

Jefferson also believed that slavery should be *abolished*, or ended. He saw that it was unnatural and unfair and that it contradicted his deep belief that all men are created equal. "The whole commerce between master and slave is a perpetual exercise of the . . . most unremitting despotism [tyranny]," he wrote. The Virginia legislature was not even willing to discuss this issue.

The Wartime Governor

Gradually, Jefferson became one of the most influential men in the Virginia legislature. In 1779, the legislature elected him governor. (Governors were not yet
elected by popular vote.) This was his first experience as an executive in government, and it was not an easy one.

First, under the Virginia constitution, the governor had very few powers.
Nearly all major decisions were to be made by the legislature, which was often
not in session. When it was in session, it spent most of its time debating and arguing. Second, the Revolutionary War was continuing, and the British would soon
invade Virginia. Third, the Virginia militia, made up mainly of small farmers, was
poorly trained and not prepared to fight. Because the state treasury was nearly
empty, there was little money for arms, ammunition, and food.

Jefferson spent much of his time recruiting new troops and trying as best as he could to defend the state. To make matters worse, he had to send soldiers to the northern states to be part of the Continental Army commanded by George Washington. That national army was also short of trained soldiers and supplies. Not surprisingly, the war in Virginia did not go well at first for the Americans. Many of the militia deserted. The new state capital at Richmond was captured by the British in January 1781 and burned.

The British commander, Lord Charles Cornwallis, even sent a small force to Monticello with orders to capture Jefferson. Jefferson evacuated his family first. Then he gathered a few crucial documents and escaped on horseback only five minutes before the enemy troops overran the hilltop.

Fast Facts

AMERICAN REVOLUTION

What: Also known as the War of Independence

When: 1776–1783

Who: Great Britain against the thirteen North American colonies, which were aided by France, the Netherlands, and Spain

Where: In the thirteen North American colonies and in the Atlantic Ocean

Why: British internal taxes and trade policies violated colonists' rights, so the colonists claimed their independence. The British found this unacceptable.

Outcome: U.S. and French armies accepted the surrender of a large British force at Yorktown, Virginia, in 1781, ending the major fighting. In the Treaty of Paris, signed in 1783, Britain recognized the independence of the American states, confirmed American fishing rights off Newfoundland, and ceded territory between the Appalachian Mountains and the Mississippi River. The United States agreed to try to end ill treatment of colonists who remained loyal to Britain by state and local governments and to restore property that had been taken from the loyalists during the war.

Fortunately, help was on the way. In the fall, Cornwallis's army took a position at Yorktown, Virginia, just a few miles from Williamsburg. A powerful fleet of French warships soon appeared off the shore at Yorktown. Then American and French armies from the north took up positions around the town. The British army was trapped, unable to escape by land or sea. In October 1781, Cornwallis surrendered his army to George Washington. This was the last major battle of the war. Within months, British and American diplomats began to negotiate a peace treaty in Paris. In a long test of courage and determination, the former colonies had defeated Great Britain and won their independence.

Thinking and Writing

Jefferson was proud of the new nation's remarkable victory. At the same time, he looked forward to returning to private life. At the end of his term as governor, he went back to Monticello. There he began to write a book that was very different from his political writings. It was called *Notes on the State of Virginia*, and it describes in great detail the plants, animals, forests, climate, history, and laws of the state. It was a grown man's version of the notebooks he kept as a boy, revealing his wide-ranging curiosity and his deep knowledge of the natural world and of politics and government.

Jefferson's book *Notes on the State of Virginia* was read and admired in the United States and Europe. It offered a wide range of informed knowledge about his home state and surrounding regions.

In the political sections of the book, Jefferson offered his opinions on the issues of the day. For example, he warned his countrymen, who were still wrestling with how to organize the new government, not to assign too much power to the legislature. An individual can become corrupt in high office, he said, but so can a legislature. "One hundred and seventy-three despots would surely be as oppressive as one," he wrote. "Human nature is the same on every side of the Atlantic, and will alike be influenced by the same courses. The time to guard against corruption and tyranny is before they shall have gotten hold of us."

Jefferson's book on Virginia and his other writings were read in Europe and the rest of the United States as well as in Virginia. Noted European thinkers and writers came to see him as an intellectual as well as political leader of the new nation. He wrestled with major social, political, and moral issues of the day, and seemed to give voice to the aspirations, or hopes and dreams, of the new American nation. The architect of Monticello was becoming an architect of a new kind of society—one based on freedom and equality.

Family Tragedy

While he was writing *Notes on the State of Virginia*, Jefferson suffered a devastating tragedy. His wife Martha died on September 6, 1782, after a long illness. She was only 33 years old. Jefferson recorded in his journal, "My dear wife died this day at 11:45 A.M." He sank into a deep depression. According to his eldest daughter, Martha (whom he called Patsy), "He kept [stayed in] his room [for] three weeks and I was never a moment from his side. He walked almost incessantly night and day, only lying down occasionally when . . . completely exhausted. . . . When at last he left his room, he rode out, and from that time he was incessantly on horseback, rambling about the mountain, in the least frequented roads, and just as often through the woods."

Now 39 years old, Jefferson was a widower with three daughters. Martha was ten, Maria was four, and Lucy was still a baby.

Congressman and Diplomat

Partly to distract himself from his grief over his wife's death, Jefferson once again entered public service. In June 1783, he allowed his Virginia colleagues to appoint him to the national Congress. The former colonies were operating under the Articles of Confederation, and the Congress was the main decision-making body.

Jefferson served only a few months, from November 1783 to May 1784, but as always, he urged the legislators to think along new lines and plan for the future. He proposed the formation of several new frontier states and devised a new monetary system for the new nation. In the British system, which the

Americans had long used, 12 pence equaled a shilling and 20 shillings equaled a pound. Jefferson said the system was too difficult. Instead, he said, American money should use the easier decimal system—100 cents (or pennies) to a dollar. On this, Congress agreed and established the units of currency that have been standard ever since.

In May 1784, Congress asked Jefferson to represent the United States in Europe. There he helped to negotiate commercial treaties with several nations, including Italy and states in present-day Germany. He lived in Paris, and in May of the following year he became the U.S. *minister* to France, the official representative of the U.S. government, taking the place of Benjamin Franklin. In his five-year stay in France, Jefferson became acquainted with its leading thinkers, scientists, and statesmen. He also witnessed the opening events of the French Revolution in July 1789. More than other Americans of his time, Jefferson found himself at home with the culture of Europe. He had grown up in the courtly society of Virginia planters, he knew European philosophy and literature, and he enjoyed music and the visual arts.

Late in 1789, Jefferson sailed for home, hoping once again to return to private life. But a few months after his arrival, he was called once again to serve the nation. The new United States Constitution had just been approved, and

Thomas Jefferson
A Philosopher a Patriote and a Friend
Dessiné par son Ami Tadée Kosciuszko.
Et Gravé par Mr. Sokolnicki.

This profile of Jefferson was drawn by his friend, the Polish patriot Tadeusz Kosciuszko, who fought with the Continental Army during the Revolutionary War and later campaigned for Polish independence.

George Washington had been chosen the nation's first president. Washington asked Jefferson to become secretary of state—the official in the new government responsible for affairs with foreign nations. Reluctantly, Jefferson agreed.

During Jefferson's years as secretary of state, he became the leader of a "faction" in the government that supported the French Revolution, in which the French had deposed their king and set up a republic. An opposing faction was led by the secretary of the treasury, Alexander Hamilton. Hamilton and his followers were horrified at the violence and destruction taking place in France. They believed that the United States should keep closer ties with Great Britain.

The factions also disagreed about the form the new government should take. Jefferson's group, which came to be known as the Democratic-Republicans, was suspicious of the power of the new federal government. Its members favored leaving most powers to the individual states. They saw the future of the country in the small landowners and farmers who could be trusted to govern themselves and settle most matters locally. Hamilton's faction, known as the Federalists, believed the federal government needed to be strengthened and that it should support industry and foreign and domestic trade.

The disagreements became so heated during Washington's second term as president that both Jefferson and Hamilton resigned their positions in the government. In the spring of 1794, Jefferson returned to Monticello, believing that he had more than fulfilled his duty to the government.

Service as Vice President

Much as Jefferson enjoyed Monticello, he was still at the center of the Democratic-Republicans, who were becoming one of the two main political parties. His supporters urged him to run for president in 1796, when Washington would be retiring, against Federalist candidate John Adams.

In elections at that time, each state chose electors, who then met to vote for the president. In 1796, more Federalist electors were chosen than Democratic-Republicans, so John Adams was elected president. But each elector got two votes. Because the Federalists split their second votes between several candidates, Thomas Jefferson finished second. This meant that he was elected vice president of the United States.

Jefferson was in an uncomfortable position. He and Adams had become friends when both were serving in Europe, and now he was Adams's vice president and back-up man. Yet as leader of the Democratic-Republican Party, Jefferson was also the head of the opposition to the new president's party. Adams suggested that he and Jefferson put aside their party affiliations and agree to work

Jefferson (above) and Hamilton (right) were the two leading members of President Washington's cabinet. Their conflicting beliefs led to the establishment of the first two political parties in the United States.

together in a nonpartisan way. Jefferson's followers were depending on him for leadership, however, so he turned down Adams's suggestion.

As the French Revolution became more intense, the differences between the parties grew and political debate became more heated. Then, in 1798, France insulted the United States by secretly demanding a bribe and a huge loan as a price for diplomatic discussions. Many people, even Democratic-Republicans, began clamoring for war against France.

During this confusing time, the Federalists in Congress, urged on by Alexander Hamilton, passed the laws known as the Alien and Sedition Acts. The Alien Act allowed the president to *deport*, or expel from the country, any non-citizen he felt was dangerous to its security. The Sedition Act made it illegal to criticize the president or the Congress openly.

Jefferson was outraged by these new laws, which he felt gave the government tyrannical powers. In a letter to James Madison, he declared that both acts were "in the teeth of the Constitution," meaning that they violated the freedoms guaranteed in that document.

Jefferson fought hard to overturn the Alien and Sedition Acts. But he found that the Democratic-Republicans lacked the votes in Congress to repeal them. Even so, this battle over freedom of speech and the threat of tyranny would soon have important consequences. For the first time in decades, Jefferson was not thinking about leaving the public stage and settling down at Monticello. Instead, he was convinced that he must save the country by ousting the Federalists from power. To do so, he must run for president again, and this time he must win.

Chapter 4

The Election of 1800

The presidential election was one of the most bitter and mean-spirited in the nation's history. Both the Federalists and Democratic-Republicans attacked each other viciously in public speeches and the press. One Federalist-leaning newspaper warned that if Jefferson and his followers won, there would be a civil war. "Murder," it said, "along with robbery, rape, adultery, and incest will be openly taught and practiced, the air will be rent with the cries of distress, the soil will be soaked with blood, and the nation black with crimes."

Jefferson himself became the main target of a poisonous press. Federalist writers accused him of treason for opposing the Alien and Sedition Acts. They claimed that he had tried to overthrow the government and make himself dictator; that he intended to eliminate all property rights; that he was a secret agent working for French dictator Napoleon Bonaparte; that he had robbed friends and widows and pocketed the money; and that he was an atheist who wanted to destroy all churches. One newspaper wrote,

> At the present solemn moment the only question to be asked by every American, laying his hand on his heart, is Shall I continue in allegiance to GOD—AND A RELIGIOUS PRESIDENT; or impiously declare for JEFFERSON—AND NO GOD!!!"

Jefferson chose not to dignify the attacks against him by replying to them. Moreover, he did not personally engage in such lying and mudslinging. Like all other candidates of the time, he stayed home during the campaign and made no public speeches. Other party members on both sides campaigned energetically in person and through printed materials, arguing the issues and examining the candidates. When voters came out to choose electors for president and vice president in November 1800, the Democratic-Republicans won a solid majority. One of the reasons was Jefferson. Even after all the personal attacks, many voters and political leaders agreed with him and trusted his judgment.

When the electors cast their votes, however, there was another big surprise. The Democratic-Republican electors were so loyal to the party that they all cast one vote for Jefferson and one for the party's vice presidential

During the campaign of 1800, the Federalists sharply criticized Jefferson's views. In this drawing he is shown kneeling at the "Altar to Gallic [French] Despotism," behind which the devil lurks. The angry American eagle is about to claw Jefferson's face.

candidate, Aaron Burr of New York. According to the Constitution, this tie would be broken by a vote in the House of Representatives, each state receiving one vote. Through 35 ballots, Democratic-Republicans voted for Jefferson and Federalists made trouble by voting for Burr. Neither candidate could win a majority. Finally, on the 36th ballot, a few Federalists, led by Jefferson's old enemy Alexander Hamilton, *abstained* (did not vote for either candidate), and Jefferson won the election. At the age of 57, he had achieved the highest office in the country he had helped to create. By placing second in the voting, Burr became vice president.

Jefferson States His Principles

Jefferson was the first president to be inaugurated in the new capital, now called Washington. On March 4, 1801, he sat on a raised platform in the Senate chamber of the new capitol building. Aaron Burr sat on his right; the new chief justice of the Supreme Court, John Marshall, sat on his left.

Before Marshall administered the oath of office, the president-elect delivered his inaugural address, now seen as one of the greatest speeches in American history. "We are all Republicans—we are all Federalists," he asserted, hoping to foster unity between the warring political parties. Then he listed the issues and principles he deemed most important. Among these were:

The States During the Presidency of Thomas Jefferson

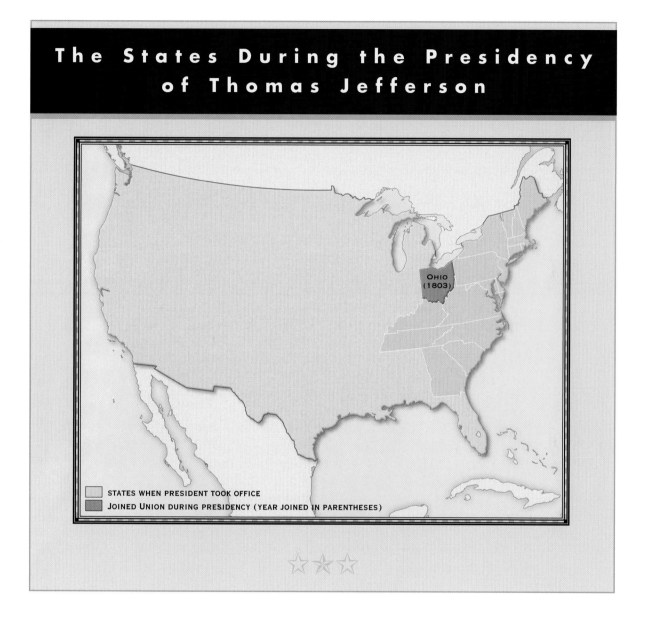

OHIO
(1803)

STATES WHEN PRESIDENT TOOK OFFICE

JOINED UNION DURING PRESIDENCY (YEAR JOINED IN PARENTHESES)

Equal and exact justice to all men, of whatever state or persuasion, religious or political; peace, commerce, and honest friendship with all nations . . . the supremacy of the civil over the military authority . . . the honest payment of our debts and sacred preservation of the public faith; encouragement of agriculture . . . freedom of religion; freedom of the press; freedom of person . . . and trial by juries impartially selected. These principles . . . should be the creed of our political faith . . . and should we wander from them in moments of error or alarm, let us hasten to retrace our steps and to regain the road which alone leads to peace, liberty, and safety.

Jefferson's emphasis on freedom of press and person signaled his intention to launch another assault on the Alien and Sedition Acts. Under his leadership, the Democratic-Republican Congress repealed them or allowed them to expire, making it safe once again for people to speak out against the government. The new president also pardoned those who had been imprisoned under the Sedition Act and even gave them letters of apology. In addition, Jefferson rolled back other Federalist policies, including some heavy taxes. True to his political philosophy, he cut back on federal actions so that the states could govern with as little interference as possible from the federal government.

A President in Carpet Slippers

Jefferson brought informal dress and customs to the White House. Presidents Washington and Adams had been formal and courtly. Jefferson wished to emphasize republican values of simplicity and the idea that the president was a servant of the people, so he did not dress up to meet visitors. On one occasion, he was criticized for wearing carpet slippers when receiving guests. He also ended the use of formal place cards and special seating at state dinners.

Jefferson was determined to do away with elaborate ceremonies. Even at his inauguration, he had no procession or parade, arriving at the Capitol alone on his own horse.

More Accusations

Jefferson's political rivals in the Federalist Party continued to attack him, taking advantage of the free press. In 1802, a resentful newspaper writer named James Callender published a series of sensational accusations in a Richmond newspaper. He claimed that Jefferson made improper advances to a married woman when he was a young man. In addition, he claimed that Jefferson had fathered at least one child with a slave woman, Sally Hemings, at Monticello.

The Sally Hemings Claims

Long after Jefferson's death, some descendants of Sally Hemings continued to claim that Thomas Jefferson was one of their ancestors. In 1974, a book by Fawn Brodie about Jefferson's private life raised the issue once again. Then in 1998, Dr. Eugene Foster published a scientific article in the journal *Nature*. He had performed DNA tests on descendants of the Jefferson and Hemings families and reported that at least one of Sally Hemings's children was fathered by someone in the Jefferson family—by Jefferson himself or perhaps by his brother or one of his nephews, who lived nearby.

These claims caused serious disagreements among Jefferson scholars and admirers. Some came to agree that Jefferson was probably the father of some or all of Hemings's children. Others found the evidence unconvincing and claimed that such conduct on Jefferson's part went against his most deeply held beliefs. The dispute may never be decided with certainty.

★★☆

Jefferson refused to make any public statements about these charges, hoping that people would eventually forget about them. Yet the stories continued to appear throughout his presidency and the rest of his life. In private letters, he confessed to friends that he had acted dishonorably as a young man but had made apologies to the married woman and her husband. He never mentioned the accusations about his relationship with Sally Hemings directly.

Expanding the United States

Even in the face of these accusations, Jefferson remained a strong and popular president. In 1801, the pasha of Tripoli, a country on the Mediterranean coast of North Africa, began firing on United States merchant ships. He demanded large sums of money as "tribute" to leave U.S. ships alone. When the government refused to pay, he declared war. After the Tripoli pirates seized the U.S. warship *Philadelphia* in 1803, President Jefferson ordered the USS *Constitution* and other warships to open fire on Tripoli. After several weeks the city surrendered, and a treaty signed in 1805 provided some protection for American shipping in the Mediterranean. The battles provided valuable training for U.S. military units. Many years later, the U.S. Marines' anthem mentioned their battles on "the shores of Tripoli."

After pirates from North Africa burned the American ship *Philadelphia*, Jefferson ordered the bombardment of the North African port of Tripoli, in present-day Libya.

The greatest achievement of Jefferson's first term, however, involved daring and skill in diplomacy. In 1800, Spain, which controlled the port of New Orleans at the mouth of the Mississippi River, secretly ceded the city and vast lands to the west of the river to France, then led by the military dictator Napoleon. When Jefferson learned of the transfer in 1802, he was deeply concerned. Spain had long allowed American farmers and trappers to transport their goods to New Orleans for shipment to the rest of the world. It seemed likely that Napoleon and the French would cut off this important gateway to world markets. Napoleon was an empire builder, and he might also seek to establish a French colony in the huge Louisiana Territory.

In the spring of 1803, Jefferson sent James Monroe, formerly governor of Virginia, to France with instructions to offer to buy the port of New Orleans from the French. By this time, Napoleon was fighting costly wars in Europe and badly needed money to support his operations. To Monroe's surprise, he offered to sell not just New Orleans, but the entire Louisiana Territory. Monroe and Robert R. Livingston, the U.S. minister to France, agreed on April 30 that the United States would buy the territory for 80 million francs—about 15 million dollars.

In October 1803, the U.S. Senate approved the Louisiana Purchase. In a single stroke, the United States had increased in size from about 900,000 to 1,700,000 square miles (2,330,000 to 4,400,000 square kilometers). Millions of acres had been obtained for about three cents each! Jefferson wrote,

> [the Mississippi River's] waters secure an independent outlet for the produce of the western states . . . free from collision with other powers. . . . [The] fertility of the country [i.e., Louisiana], its climate and extent [large size] promise in due season [to become] important aids to our treasury [and] an ample provision for our posterity [future generations].

Napoleon Bonaparte was a military hero and unchallenged leader of France in 1803, when he agreed to sell the Louisiana Territory to the United States.

The Louisiana Purchase

The Louisiana Territory included all or part of 15 present-day states.

ALL OF: Oklahoma, Arkansas, Kansas, Missouri, Nebraska, Iowa

MOST OF: Louisiana, Colorado, Wyoming, Montana, South Dakota, Minnesota

PARTS OF: Texas, New Mexico, North Dakota

In this early map, the Louisiana Purchase includes all of present-day Texas. However, Texas remained under the control of Spain, and later Mexico, until 1836, and became part of the United States only in 1845.

Even if the Louisiana Purchase had been Jefferson's only achievement as president, it would have been enough to rank him among the greatest.

The Lewis and Clark Expedition

Even before the Louisiana Purchase, Jefferson had become curious about the vast lands west of the Mississippi. What was the nature of the lands? Was there a water passage to the Pacific Ocean? He discussed these questions with his secretary, Meriwether Lewis. An intelligent officer with ten or twelve chosen men, Jefferson said, might explore the region, all the way to the Pacific Ocean.

Lewis and Clark met and dealt peacefully with many tribes of Native Americans on their long expedition up the Missouri River and west to the Pacific.

When the purchase was made, Jefferson quickly gained funding for an expedition and asked Meriwether Lewis to organize it. Lewis recruited an old army friend, Captain William Clark, who shared command. Their instructions were to search for a water route to the Pacific Ocean and to record information about the Indian tribes, animals, plants, and weather they encountered along the way.

Toward the Far Horizon

Leaving St. Louis on May 14, 1804, the Lewis and Clark expedition traveled up the Missouri River and reached central North Dakota by November. They wintered there and resumed their trek toward the far horizon in the spring of 1805. A Shoshone Indian woman, Sacajawea, accompanied them to help communicate with western tribes. They crossed the Rocky Mountains in August and reached the mouth of the Columbia River and Pacific Ocean in November 1805.

In March 1806, the expedition headed for home and reached St. Louis on September 23, 1806. Their incredible journey covered more than 8,000 miles (12,800 km), and they brought back a vast store of information that would be priceless not only to later explorers and settlers, but to natural scientists. In decades to come, hundreds of thousands of Americans would follow the expedition westward across the continent, settling vast tracts of the huge new territory.

☆ ☆ ☆

Chapter 5

A New Vice President ———————

Although Jefferson had originally planned to serve only one term as president, in 1804, with a new election looming, he changed his mind. On the one hand, his supporters strongly urged him to run again. His first administration had been a tremendous success, they said, and the nation needed him to keep it going in the right direction. Jefferson might have brushed aside such flattery and retired to Monticello, but he knew that the Federalists wanted badly to regain power. He believed that they still posed a threat to the country's democratic ideals, so he agreed to run for a second term.

One of his first tasks was to choose a new candidate for vice president. Jefferson had not trusted Vice President Aaron Burr from the beginning of his administration, and had not consulted him on important matters. In 1804, Burr ran unsuccessfully for governor of

New York. During the heated campaign, he was severely criticized by Alexander Hamilton, leader of the Federalists. Burr challenged Hamilton to a duel to defend his honor. Duels were illegal, but on July 11, they met in Weehawken, New Jersey, just across the Hudson River from New York City. Hamilton's shot missed, but Burr's found its target, and Hamilton died of his wounds the next day.

Jefferson's rival Alexander Hamilton and his vice president Aaron Burr fought a duel in Weehawken, New Jersey, in 1804. Hamilton died of his wounds. Burr avoided prosecution for dueling and served out the rest of his term as vice president.

Hamilton was nearly as brilliant and accomplished as Jefferson himself, and he had contributed greatly to the establishment of the United States. Yet the two men had been fierce political opponents for many years and were founders of the two major political parties of the day. They were the two most effective spokesmen for differing views of the American government and the Constitution. When Hamilton died, Jefferson lost his most able opponent. The Federalist party lost its most accomplished leader.

Jefferson chose New York's George Clinton as the Democratic-Republican candidate for vice president in place of Aaron Burr. The ticket won a landslide victory over the Federalist candidates, Charles C. Pinckney and Rufus King. In his moment of triumph, Jefferson had no way of knowing that Burr would soon make a bizarre comeback that would actually threaten the country's security.

High Hopes at the Second Inaugural ——————

Jefferson looked toward his second term with optimism. In his second inaugural address, delivered on March 4, 1805, he reviewed the record of accomplishments of his first term. In addition to his victory over the pirates of Tripoli and the Louisiana Purchase, he had eliminated numerous burdensome taxes while greatly increasing the size of the U.S. treasury. Jefferson proposed using the funds for an ambitious program of internal improvements. These would include "rivers, canals, roads, arts, manufactures, education, and other great objects within each state."

Jefferson also addressed the campaign of lies and distortions waged by Federalist opponents and the newspapers. He fervently believed in a free press and opposed government censorship, confident that truth would, of its own strength, overcome falsehood in the end:

> Since truth and reason have maintained their ground against false
> opinions in league with false facts, the press, confined to truth, needs
> no other legal restraint; the public judgment will correct false reasoning
> and opinions, on a full hearing of all parties.

A Desire to Avoid War

Despite Jefferson's hopes, his second term did not go smoothly. Personal attacks continued. Also, the large surplus in the federal treasury was swallowed up by military spending, making his public works programs impossible. The main recurring theme of these four years was Jefferson's efforts to keep the country out of the destructive wars then sweeping Europe.

The most dangerous of the wars was the long struggle between Britain and France. Napoleon, who had sold Louisiana to the United States, was preparing to invade Britain. In the Atlantic and other waterways, French and British ships challenged each other, and both countries claimed the right to capture any foreign vessels that might be supplying the other side.

The United States was caught in the middle. It needed to keep up trade with these two powerful nations, but if it sided with one, it would lose trade with the other. Worse, when French or British ships stopped and searched U.S. merchant ships, people at home wanted to fight the offending side. Jefferson realized that becoming entangled in a major war could seriously weaken or even destroy the country. So he made every effort to avoid being drawn into the conflict.

Outrages on the High Seas

As the British lost many sailors to battle or desertion, they began seizing American ships and *impressing* American sailors, or forcing them into service on British ships. Then in 1806 and 1807, Britain and France imposed blockades on each other, trying to keep foreign goods from reaching the other side. American vessels caught in either British or French waters would be stopped and seized. Cut off from nearly all trade with Europe, American farmers and merchants began to suffer. They demanded that the United States defend itself, by war if necessary.

In June 1807, the American warship *Chesapeake* was cruising off the coast of Virginia when it encountered the British warship *Leopard*. The captain of the *Leopard* believed the *Chesapeake* was harboring a British deserter and demanded to be allowed to board and search it. The American captain refused, and the *Leopard* opened fire, heavily damaging the American ship. Then the British boarded the *Chesapeake*. They seized the deserter and took two American sailors. When news of the incident spread through the United States, calls for war against Britain reached a fever pitch.

After the U.S. ship *Constitution* was damaged by British fire and boarded by British sailors, its officers (left) offer their swords to the British commander as a sign they have been defeated in battle. The British commander refuses to take them.

The Embargo Act

Jefferson, hoping to avoid war, tried to negotiate a settlement with the British over the impressment of American sailors. When this failed, he cautiously went ahead with a military buildup, proposing that hundreds of gunboats be built. He also suggested the construction of submarines equipped with torpedoes to destroy British ships if they invaded U.S. waters. Like many of Jefferson's inventive ideas, this one was far ahead of its time. More practical men refused to take the idea seriously.

Another strategy Jefferson devised was to impose restrictions on British and French trade. In December 1807, he proposed the Embargo Act, which Congress passed. It kept ships bound for any foreign nation from leaving from American ports. Jefferson hoped to keep American grain, cotton, and manufactured goods from Britain and France and their allies, believing this embargo would force them to deal more fairly with the United States.

The embargo proved a failure, however. Thousands of American merchants and sailors lost their jobs. Farm prices dropped, and many farmers went bankrupt because they could not sell their crops at a profit. The embargo ended up hurting the United States more than it hurt Europe.

Despite the economic problems created by the embargo and the looming threat of war, Jefferson remained steadfast in his desire to maintain peace. In a speech delivered in February 1808, he said:

Merchants and sailors were badly hurt by the embargo, and Jefferson's opponents ridiculed it. In this cartoon, the embargo is shown as a terrapin (or snapping turtle) biting a merchant. The merchant calls the terrapin "Ograbme," which is "embargo" spelled backward.

So fortunately remote from the theater of European contests, and carefully avoiding to implicate ourselves in them, we had a right to hope for an exemption [immunity] from the calamities which have afflicted the contending nations, and to be permitted . . . to pursue paths of industry and peace.

As he was leaving office in March 1809, Jefferson reluctantly repealed the embargo for all nations except Britain and France.

Burr's Fantastic Scheme

Even as Jefferson and his advisers worked to avoid overseas conflicts, events at home suddenly became threatening. Bitter over his fall from political office, Aaron Burr began plotting to achieve power and glory. He planned secretly to raise a small army of westerners unhappy with the national government. He would drive out the Spanish settlers still lingering in Louisiana and march on Mexico, then a colony of Spain. With Mexico as part of his empire, he could conquer some western U.S. states and become the ruler of a new empire that could challenge the United States for control of North America. "The gods invite us to glory and fortune," he told fellow conspirator James Wilkinson.

Apparently the gods did not favor Burr's venture. Jefferson learned of the plot, and Wilkinson provided an incriminating letter. The president saw Burr as a traitor, and on November 27, 1806, he issued a proclamation exposing the conspiracy. Burr's support vanished, and Burr himself was held for trial. Jefferson wrote a friend:

> This affair has been a great confirmation in my mind of the innate
> strength of the form of our government. He had probably induced near a
> thousand men to engage with him by making them believe the
> government [was involved in] it. A proclamation alone, by undeceiving
> them, so completely disarmed him, that he had not above thirty men left.

Aaron Burr, no longer in office, planned to invade regions in the south and west and may have hoped to form a new country with himself as ruler. Jefferson publicized the conspiracy and it soon collapsed. Burr was tried on charges of treason and acquitted.

Most people believed Burr was guilty of treason, but the conspiracy was difficult to prove in court. "Such are the jealous provisions of our laws in favor of the accused, and against the accuser, that I question if he can be convicted," Jefferson wrote. He was right. Chief Justice Marshall required more evidence than the prosecutors could offer. Burr was acquitted and fled to Europe.

The Shackles of Power

Jefferson had succeeded in keeping the country out of war overseas and defended it against conspiracy at home. But the Embargo Act had brought hard times to the country, and many of his hopes for his second term were not realized. Jefferson himself was tired. Nearly 66 years old, he had served in the government almost continuously for 20 years. He was eager to retire.

The Democratic-Republican Party was strong and well prepared for a change. James Madison, who had served Jefferson for eight years as secretary of state, became its candidate for president, and in November of 1808, he was elected by a comfortable margin and prepared to take office the following March.

On March 4, 1809, Jefferson rode alone on his horse to the Capitol to witness his longtime friend James Madison sworn in as the nation's fourth president. After congratulating the new leader, Jefferson returned to the White House to finish packing his belongings. On March 11, he quietly struck out for

Thank God for Retirement

On March 2, 1809, Jefferson wrote to a French acquaintance:

Within a few days I retire to my family, my books, and farms. . . . Never did a prisoner, released from his chains, feel such relief as I shall on shaking off the shackles of power. Nature intended me for the tranquil pursuits of science, by rendering them my supreme delight. But the enormities of the times in which I have lived have forced me to take part in resisting them, and to commit myself on the boisterous ocean of political passions. I thank God for the opportunity of retiring from them.

★★☆

Monticello. A few days before, a major newspaper had written, "Never will it be forgotten as long as liberty is dear to man that it was on this day that Thomas Jefferson retired from the supreme magistracy [the nation's highest office] amidst the blessings and regrets of millions."

Chapter 6

Welcome Home

When Jefferson reached Monticello in mid-March 1809, he enjoyed an especially warm welcome. His daughter Martha, grandchildren, and slaves were waiting for him. They crowded around him as he made his way along the road that wound uphill to the house. As he stepped through the front door, a happy realization swept over him. He was home to stay at last.

Indeed, in the next 17 years, Jefferson rarely ventured far from the estate. Yet he remained as busy as ever, applying his energy and intellect to agricultural and educational projects, inventions, and improvements. He kept in touch with his many friends and allies by letter-writing on a grand scale. He seemed to be making up for lost time. After all, the duties of public service had caused him to miss many years of private pursuits on his beloved hilltop.

Jefferson returned to Monticello in 1809, where he lived for the rest of his life. Even today, Monticello blooms with flowers from early spring through the summer and fall.

Gardener, Inventor, and Grandfather ———

One of Jefferson's first projects was gardening, which brought him much pleasure and relaxation. "No occupation is so delightful to me as the culture of the earth," he said, "and no culture comparable to that of the garden." One of his granddaughters later recalled, "When he first returned to Monticello, [he] immediately began to prepare new beds for his flowers." He also created experimental food gardens all around the estate, testing new crops and new ways of cultivating them. He sent descriptions of his efforts, along with seeds, clippings, and samples, to local farmers. Among the crops he planted were rice, figs, pecans, walnuts, corn, apricots, and strawberries.

Jefferson also devoted many hours to inventing or improving on work-saving and timesaving devices. One was a *dumbwaiter*, a small mechanical elevator that transported wine bottles and other supplies from the basement to the dining room. He was particularly fond of the *polygraph*, created by John Isaac Hawkins. It was a writing machine consisting of five pens attached to mechanical bars and levers. When a person wrote with one pen, the others duplicated the letters and words, producing copies. It was a distant ancestor of the photocopy machine and allowed Jefferson to keep copies of the many letters he sent to others. He called it a most precious invention.

Among Jefferson's ingenious gadgets at Monticello was a dumbwaiter — a small elevator hidden in the mantle of this fireplace to carry wines and food from the basement up to the main floor.

Much of the former president's time also went to his grandchildren, of whom twelve lived with him at Monticello at one time or another. His granddaughter Virginia later remembered:

His cheerfulness and affection were the warm sun in which his family all basked. . . . Cheerfulness, love, benevolence, wisdom, seemed to animate his whole form. His face beamed with them. . . . I looked on him as being too great and good for my comprehension. . . . When he walked in the garden and would call the children to go with him, we raced after and before him. . . . I never heard him utter a harsh word to one of us . . . or use a threat. He simply said, "Do," or "Do not." . . . One of our earliest amusements was in running races on the terrace, or around the lawn. He placed us according to our ages, giving the youngest and smallest the [head] start of all the others by some yards. . . . Our reward [was] dried fruit—three figs, prunes, or dates to the victor, two to the second, and one to the [one] who came in last.

Of the grandchildren, Jefferson became especially close to Martha's son, Thomas Jefferson Randolph, whom he called Jeff. Gradually, as the young man matured, Jefferson entrusted him with managing the estate and his affairs.

A portrait of Jefferson by Rembrandt Peale shows him wearing a distinctive fur collar.

Builder and Champion of Learning ————

Another project that filled many of Jefferson's days was the expansion and improvement of Monticello itself. Between 1810 and 1817, he made it larger and more attractive than ever. A young visitor from Boston, George Ticknor, described how it appeared in 1815, when Jefferson was 72:

[The house] is of brick, two stories high in the wings, with a piazza [porch] in front of a receding center. You enter by a glass folding door into a hall. . . . On one side hang the head and horns of an elk, a deer, and a buffalo; another [wall] is covered with curiosities which Lewis and Clark found in their wild and perilous expedition. . . . Through this hall—or rather museum—we passed to the dining room. . . . [In the study] we found ourselves surrounded with paintings. . . . [It is] a large and rather elegant room twenty or thirty feet high, which with the hall I have described composes the whole center of the house from top to bottom. The floor of this room . . . is formed of alternate diamonds of cherry and beach [woods], and kept polished as highly as if it were of fine mahogany. [The] collection of books [in the library], now so much talked about, consists of about seven thousand volumes, contained in a

The large windows and high ceilings at Monticello provide natural light and make the rooms seem airy and spacious.

suite of fine rooms; and is arranged in the catalogue and on the shelves according to the divisions and subdivisions of human learning.

Later in 1815, Jefferson made the contents of this extraordinary private library, then the largest in North America, public property. In 1800, Congress had created the Library of Congress, in Washington, D.C. In 1814, during the War of 1812, the British overran Washington and burned many public buildings. The collection of the Library was destroyed. So in 1815, Jefferson generously offered to sell Congress his personal library for $24,000. His own collection became the nucleus of what is now the world's largest library.

Jefferson also continued his crusade to advance the cause of learning in other ways. During his years in the White House, he had called for the creation of a modern university supported by public funds. Now, though he was elderly and retired, he took on this huge task by himself. The state legislature agreed to locate a state-supported university in Charlottesville, not far from Monticello. Between 1814 and 1815, Jefferson helped raise the needed funds, designed the main buildings, and even formulated a *curriculum*, or plan of courses to be taught. The University of Virginia was chartered in 1819 and opened in 1825.

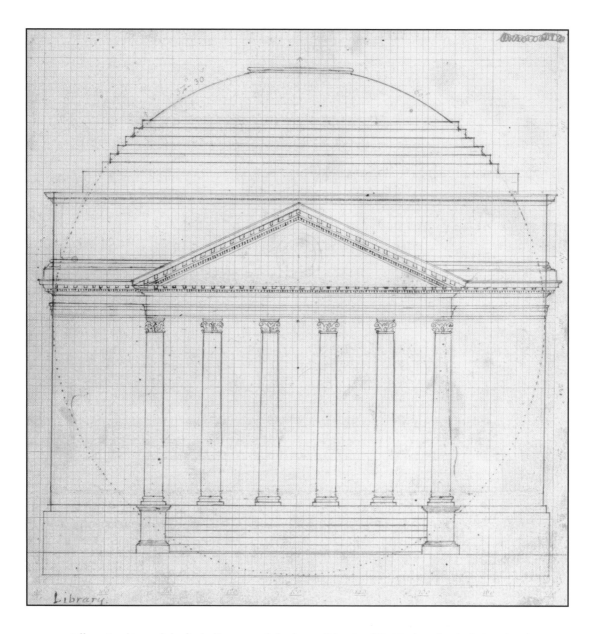

Jefferson's architectural plan for the library rotunda for the new University of Virginia shows that the design is based on a circle. The photograph at right shows the rotunda today.

Keeping in Touch

Jefferson wrote dozens of letters each week. Jeff Randolph reckoned that his grandfather received more than 26,000 letters during his retirement and answered more than 16,000 of them. Jefferson kept in touch with James Madison and other colleagues who still served the country in Washington, D.C. He also corresponded with numerous relatives and old friends both in the United States and abroad. Writing so many letters day after day, year after year, was time-consuming and taxing and kept him, in his own words, "at the drudgery of the writing-table all the prime hours of the day." This left him little time for reading.

Jefferson even reached out to old opponents. John Adams and Jefferson had become friends in the 1780s, when both were serving in France. But they later disagreed over political theories, and the bitterness of the 1800 election (in which Jefferson defeated Adams) had driven a wedge of silence between them. In 1812, Adams finally broke the ice and sent a letter to Monticello. Overjoyed, Jefferson answered, "No circumstances have . . . suspended for one moment my sincere esteem for you, and I now salute you with unchanged affection and respect." In the next 14 years, the two men exchanged more than 150 letters covering a wide range of topics. One modern historian calls it the greatest correspondence between prominent statesmen in all of American history.

Dreams of the Future

In their long correspondence, Jefferson and Adams sometimes compared the country they had helped to create to those in Europe. In a letter dated August 1, 1816, Jefferson told his friend:

Bigotry is the disease of ignorance, of morbid minds. . . . Education and free discussion are the antidotes of both. We [i.e., the United States] are destined to be a barrier against the returns of ignorance and barbarism. Old Europe will have to lean on our shoulders, and to hobble along by our side . . . as [best] she can. . . . I like the dreams of the future better than the history of the past, so good night! I will dream on, always fancying that . . . [you] are by my side marking the progress . . . of ages and countries.

☆☆☆

July 4, 1826

The year 1826 brought a special occasion for celebration in the United States—the 50th anniversary of the Declaration of Independence. As the year opened, two of the men on the committee that drafted the Declaration were still alive—Thomas Jefferson and John Adams. As July 4 approached, the 83-year-old Jefferson had grown so weak that he was confined to his bed. He realized that he was dying. But he desperately wanted to hold out until the anniversary on July 4. He just managed. His grandson, Jeff Randolph, remembered, "He ceased to breathe, without a struggle, fifty minutes past meridian [noon]—July 4, 1826. I closed his eyes with my own hands."

Randolph and the others at Jefferson's bedside did not yet realize that one of history's greatest coincidences was taking place. On that same day, in distant Quincy, Massachusetts, John Adams also lay on his deathbed. He, too, had managed to hold onto life until that day so special to both men. Unaware of his friend's illness, Adams said shortly before his own death, "Thomas Jefferson still survives."

On the Altar of God

Adams's words on his deathbed have become true in a different sense—Jefferson still lives. His ideas and accomplishments had a huge impact not only on his generation but on the course of the world over nearly 200 years. He set down ideals of freedom and equality in moving phrases that still stir people's hearts, guiding the United States and affecting governments and people in every corner of the world. In 1776, the United States was the world's only republican government dedicated to individual rights. Today there are many, and the number continues to grow, fulfilling Jefferson's prediction that humanity was then awakening to a new and momentous dawn of freedom:

> All eyes are opened, or opening, to the rights of man. The general
>
> spread of the light of science has already . . . [revealed] the palpable
>
> truth, that the mass of mankind has not been born with saddles on their

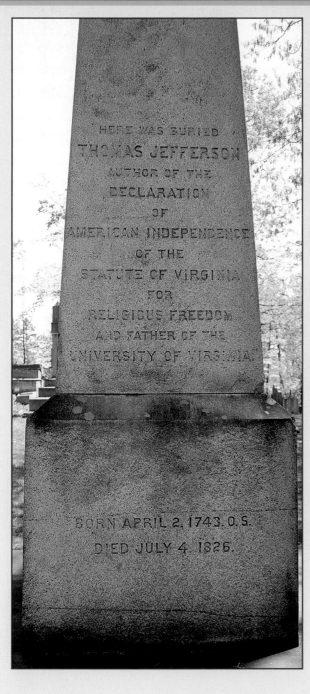

Thomas Jefferson's family buried him beside his wife, Martha, and his old friend, Dabney Carr, in the small graveyard at Monticello. They marked his headstone with the following words, written by Jefferson himself:

HERE WAS BURIED

THOMAS JEFFERSON,

AUTHOR OF THE

DECLARATION

OF

AMERICAN INDEPENDENCE,

OF THE

STATUTE OF VIRGINIA

FOR

RELIGIOUS FREEDOM,

AND FATHER OF THE

UNIVERSITY OF VIRGINIA.

He lists among his greatest accomplishments nothing that he did as president.

In Washington, D.C., a larger-than-life statue of Jefferson stands inside the Jefferson Memorial, which is built in the shape of a rotunda, recalling Jefferson's own architectural designs.

backs, nor a favored few . . . ready to ride them. . . . These are grounds
of hope for others.

No single phrase uttered by Thomas Jefferson can sum up his devotion to
human liberty and dignity and the legacy of his fight for these ideals. But this one,
carved into the Jefferson Memorial in the nation's capital, comes close:

I have sworn on the altar of God, eternal hostility against every form of
tyranny over the mind of man.

Fast Facts Thomas Jefferson

Birth:	April 13, 1743
Birthplace:	Shadwell, Albemarle County, Virginia
Parents:	Peter Jefferson and Jane Randolph Jefferson
Brothers & Sisters:	One brother and six sisters (two others died in infancy)
Education:	Graduated from the College of William and Mary, 1762. Studied law privately in Williamsburg
Occupation:	Lawyer, planter
Marriage:	To Martha Wayles Skelton, January 1, 1772
Children:	Martha Washington Jefferson (Patsy), 1772–1836
	Maria Jefferson (Polly), 1778–1804
	(four other children died in infancy)
Political Party:	Democratic-Republican
Political Offices:	1768–74 Member, Virginia House of Burgesses
	1775–76 Member, Second Continental Congress
	1779–81 Governor of Virginia
	1783–84 Member, Continental Congress
	1785–89 U.S. Minister to France
	1789–93 Secretary of State (under George Washington)
	1797–01 Vice President (under John Adams)
	1801–09 Third President of the United States
His Vice Presidents:	1801–05 Aaron Burr
	1805–09 George Clinton
Major Actions as President:	1803 Authorized attacks on Tripoli (North Africa) to end raids on U.S. ships by pirates
	1803 Authorized the Louisiana Purchase, nearly doubling the land area of the U.S.
	1803 Encouraged and approved the Lewis and Clark expedition to explore the far west
	1807 Approved the Embargo Act, prohibiting trade with Europe to retaliate against Britain and France
Firsts:	To be inaugurated president in Washington, D.C.
Death:	July 4, 1826 (former president John Adams died the same day)
Age at Death:	83 years
Burial Place:	Monticello, his estate near Charlottesville, Virginia

Fast Facts

Martha Wayles
Skelton Jefferson

Birth:	October 19, 1748
Birthplace:	Lancaster, England
Parents:	John Wayles and Martha Eppes Wayles
Education:	Home taught
Marriages:	To Balthurst Skelton, November 20, 1766 (he died in 1770)
	To Thomas Jefferson, January 1, 1772
Children:	John Skelton, 1767–1771
	Six children with Thomas Jefferson, *see* list at left
Firsts:	First future president's wife to die before he was elected
Death:	September 6, 1782
Age at Death:	34 years
Burial Place:	Monticello, the Jefferson estate near Charlottesville, Virginia

Timeline

1743	1757	1760	1762	1765
Thomas Jefferson is born at Shadwell, an estate in the British colony of Virginia.	His father, Peter, dies.	Enrolls at the College of William and Mary, in Williamsburg, Virginia.	Begins his study of law with George Wythe.	The British impose the unpopular Stamp Act on the American colonies.

1779	1781	1782	1785	1789
Jefferson proposes a bill for religious freedom in the Virginia legislature; he becomes governor of the state.	A British army surrenders to George Washington at Yorktown, Virginia, ending the war.	Martha Jefferson dies after a long illness.	Jefferson is appointed U.S. minister to France.	President George Washington appoints Jefferson secretary of state.

1804	1806	1807	1809	1812
U.S. forces defeat the Barbary pirates of North Africa; Jefferson is reelected for a second term.	Jefferson foils an attempt by Burr to conquer Mexico and create a personal empire in North America.	Americans, outraged at the *Chesapeake* incident, clamor for war against Britain; Jefferson retaliates by pushing through the Embargo Act.	Jefferson retires to Monticello. James Madison becomes president.	Jefferson resumes correspondence with John Adams after years of silence.

1768
Jefferson enters the Virginia legislature, the House of Burgesses.

1770
Begins building a new home, Monticello, on a hilltop near Shadwell.

1772
Marries Martha Wayles Skelton.

1775
The first shots of the American Revolution ring out at Concord and Lexington, in Massachusetts.

1776
The colonies declare their independence from Britain; Jefferson writes the Declaration of Independence.

1794
After resigning as secretary of state, Jefferson returns to Monticello.

1796/97
Jefferson is elected vice president under John Adams.

1800/01
Jefferson is elected president, defeating John Adams.

1803
Jefferson's agents buy the Louisiana Territory from France, doubling the area of the United States.

1803
Initiates the Lewis and Clark expedition to explore the lands beyond the Mississippi.

1814
In the War of 1812, the British capture Washington, D.C., and burn the White House and Library of Congress.

1815
Jefferson sells his personal collection of books to Congress to reestablish the Library of Congress.

1825
The University of Virginia, conceived and designed by Jefferson, opens.

1826
Jefferson dies on July 4, the 50th anniversary of the Declaration of Independence; John Adams dies the same day.

Glossary

abolish: to end

abstain: to withhold a vote

advocate: a supporter of or spokesperson for someone or something

alien: a person not born in the country; an immigrant or visitor

aristocracy: a privileged class of people

curriculum: a list of courses and subjects to be taught in a school

deport: to expel from a country

dissolve: to close down an institution

dumbwaiter: a small elevator-like device that transports goods from one floor to another

duties: taxes, especially on imported goods

impress: to force sailors of one nation into service to another

minister: the official representative of a country's government to the government of another country

Parliament: Britain's national legislature

philosophy: the study of ideas and the meaning of life

polygraph: a primitive copy machine, consisting of several pens connected to mechanical bars and levers

treason: betraying or going against one's own country

Further Reading

Bober, Natalie S. *Thomas Jefferson: Man on a Mountain.* New York: Aladdin Paperbacks, 1997.

Heinrichs, Ann. *Thomas Jefferson.* Minneapolis: Compass Point Books, 2002.

Lanier, Shannon, and Jane Feldman, *Jefferson's Children: The Story of One American Family.* New York: Random House, 2000.

Lukes, Bonnie L. *The American Revolution.* San Diego: Lucent Books, 1996.

Meltzer, Milton. *Thomas Jefferson: The Revolutionary Aristocrat.* New York: Franklin Watts, 1991.

Nardo, Don. *The Declaration of Independence: A Model for Individual Rights.* San Diego: Lucent Books, 1999.

Santella, Andrew. *Lewis and Clark.* Danbury: Franklin Watts, 2001.

Webster, Christine. *The Lewis and Clark Expedition.* Danbury: Children's Press, 2003.

Young, Robert. *A Personal Tour of Monticello.* Minneapolis: Lerner, 1999.

MORE ADVANCED READING

Ambrose, Stephen E. *Undaunted Courage: Meriwether Lewis, Thomas Jefferson, and the Opening of the American West.* New York: Simon and Schuster, 1996.

Brodie, Fawn. *Thomas Jefferson: An Intimate History.* New York: W.W. Norton, 1974.

Ellis, Joseph J. *American Sphinx: The Character of Thomas Jefferson.* New York: Knopf, 1997.

——, ed. *Thomas Jefferson: Genius of Liberty.* New York: Viking Press, 2000.

Malone, Dumas. *Jefferson the Virginian.* Boston: Little, Brown, 1948.

——. *Jefferson the President: First Term, 1801–1805.* Boston: Little, Brown, 1970.

——. *Jefferson the President: Second Term, 1805–1809.* Boston: Little Brown, 1974.

Peterson, Merrill, ed. *Thomas Jefferson: Writings.* Washington, D.C.: Library of America, 1984.

Randall, Willard S. *Thomas Jefferson: A Life.* New York: Harper-Collins, 1993.

Places to Visit

★ ★ ★ ★ ★

Monticello

P.O. Box 217

Charlottesville, VA 22902

(434) 984-9822

Jefferson's Virginia home, which he designed himself. For general information about planning the trip and the site's attractions, see "The Home of Thomas Jefferson: Monticello," at

http://www.monticello.org

Jefferson Memorial

A beautiful monument in Washington, D.C., built and dedicated to Jefferson and his legacy. For general information, see "Ben's Guide for Kids: The Jefferson Memorial," at *http://bensguide.gpo.gov/3-5/symbols/ jefferson.html*

Library of Congress

101 Independence Avenue

Washington, D.C. 20540

General information: (202) 707-5000

Visitors' information: (202) 707-8000

Located in Washington, D.C., this huge facility, which Jefferson helped establish, is the home of his personal collection of books, as well as many of his official papers. For a summary of these items, see "The Thomas Jefferson Papers at the Library of Congress," at *http://memory.loc.gov/ammem/mtjhtml/ mtjhome.html*

Online Sites of Interest

★**American Presidents**

http://www.americanpresident.org/

Provides brief biographies of each president and much additional information on his childhood, political career, presidency, and retirement.

★**Internet Public Library, Presidents of the United States (IPL POTUS)**

http://www.ipl.si.umich.edu/div/potus/tjefferson.html

Excellent resource for personal, political, historical materials about Jefferson. It includes links to other Internet sites.

★**The White House**

http://www.whitehouse.gov/WH/Welcome.html

This site provides information about the current president and vice president, a history of the Executive Mansion, virtual tours, biographies of U.S. presidents, and many other items of interest.

★**The Life of Thomas Jefferson**

http://etext.lib.virginia.edu/jefferson/biog

This excellent online biography of Jefferson, written in 1834 by B. L. Rayner, has many related links.

★**Jefferson and Sally Hemings**

http://www.angelfire.com/va/TJTruth/background.html

http://www.monticello.org/plantation/hemingscontro/hemings_resource.html

http://www.ashbrook.org/articles/mayer-hemings.html#ll

These Web sites contain information about the controversy over Jefferson and his alleged relationship with his slave, Sally Hemings.

★**The Architecture of Thomas Jefferson**

http://www.iath.virginia.edu/wilson/home.html

A site about Jefferson's architectural endeavors, with links to sites showing some of his architectural drawings.

Table of Presidents

1. George Washington

2. John Adams

3. Thomas Jefferson

4. James Madison

	1. George Washington	2. John Adams	3. Thomas Jefferson	4. James Madison
Took office	Apr 30 1789	Mar 4 1797	Mar 4 1801	Mar 4 1809
Left office	Mar 3 1797	Mar 3 1801	Mar 3 1809	Mar 3 1817
Birthplace	Westmoreland Co, VA	Braintree, MA	Shadwell, VA	Port Conway, VA
Birth date	Feb 22 1732	Oct 20 1735	Apr 13 1743	Mar 16 1751
Death date	Dec 14 1799	July 4 1826	July 4 1826	June 28 1836

9. William H. Harrison

10. John Tyler

11. James K. Polk

12. Zachary Taylor

	9. William H. Harrison	10. John Tyler	11. James K. Polk	12. Zachary Taylor
Took office	Mar 4 1841	Apr 6 1841	Mar 4 1845	Mar 5 1849
Left office	Apr 4 1841•	Mar 3 1845	Mar 3 1849	July 9 1850•
Birthplace	Berkeley, VA	Greenway, VA	Mecklenburg Co, NC	Barboursville, VA
Birth date	Feb 9 1773	Mar 29 1790	Nov 2 1795	Nov 24 1784
Death date	Apr 4 1841	Jan 18 1862	June 15 1849	July 9 1850

17. Andrew Johnson

18. Ulysses S. Grant

19. Rutherford B. Hayes

20. James A. Garfield

	17. Andrew Johnson	18. Ulysses S. Grant	19. Rutherford B. Hayes	20. James A. Garfield
Took office	Apr 15 1865	Mar 4 1869	Mar 4 1877	Mar 4 1881
Left office	Mar 3 1869	Mar 3 1877	Mar 3 1881	Sept 19 1881•
Birthplace	Raleigh, NC	Point Pleasant, OH	Delaware, OH	Orange, OH
Birth date	Dec 29 1808	Apr 27 1822	Oct 4 1822	Nov 19 1831
Death date	July 31 1875	July 23 1885	Jan 17 1893	Sept 19 1881

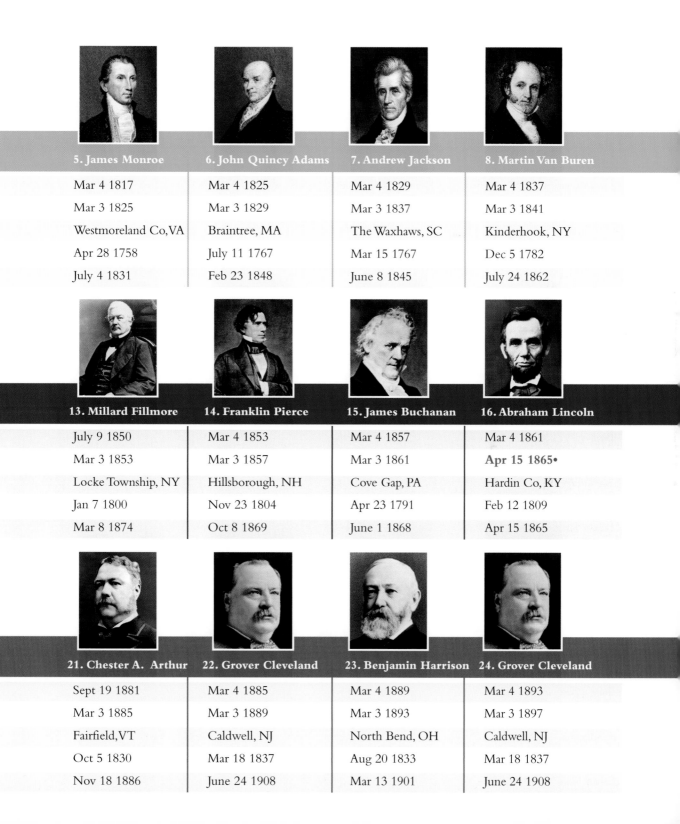

5. James Monroe

Mar 4 1817

Mar 3 1825

Westmoreland Co, VA

Apr 28 1758

July 4 1831

6. John Quincy Adams

Mar 4 1825

Mar 3 1829

Braintree, MA

July 11 1767

Feb 23 1848

7. Andrew Jackson

Mar 4 1829

Mar 3 1837

The Waxhaws, SC

Mar 15 1767

June 8 1845

8. Martin Van Buren

Mar 4 1837

Mar 3 1841

Kinderhook, NY

Dec 5 1782

July 24 1862

13. Millard Fillmore

July 9 1850

Mar 3 1853

Locke Township, NY

Jan 7 1800

Mar 8 1874

14. Franklin Pierce

Mar 4 1853

Mar 3 1857

Hillsborough, NH

Nov 23 1804

Oct 8 1869

15. James Buchanan

Mar 4 1857

Mar 3 1861

Cove Gap, PA

Apr 23 1791

June 1 1868

16. Abraham Lincoln

Mar 4 1861

Apr 15 1865•

Hardin Co, KY

Feb 12 1809

Apr 15 1865

21. Chester A. Arthur

Sept 19 1881

Mar 3 1885

Fairfield, VT

Oct 5 1830

Nov 18 1886

22. Grover Cleveland

Mar 4 1885

Mar 3 1889

Caldwell, NJ

Mar 18 1837

June 24 1908

23. Benjamin Harrison

Mar 4 1889

Mar 3 1893

North Bend, OH

Aug 20 1833

Mar 13 1901

24. Grover Cleveland

Mar 4 1893

Mar 3 1897

Caldwell, NJ

Mar 18 1837

June 24 1908

25. William McKinley

26. Theodore Roosevelt

27. William H. Taft

28. Woodrow Wilson

	25. William McKinley	26. Theodore Roosevelt	27. William H. Taft	28. Woodrow Wilson
Took office	Mar 4 1897	Sept 14 1901	Mar 4 1909	Mar 4 1913
Left office	**Sept 14 1901•**	Mar 3 1909	Mar 3 1913	Mar 3 1921
Birthplace	Niles, OH	New York, NY	Cincinnati, OH	Staunton, VA
Birth date	Jan 29 1843	Oct 27 1858	Sept 15 1857	Dec 28 1856
Death date	Sept 14 1901	Jan 6 1919	Mar 8 1930	Feb 3 1924

	33. Harry S. Truman	34. Dwight D. Eisenhower	35. John F. Kennedy	36. Lyndon B. Johnson
Took office	Apr 12 1945	Jan 20 1953	Jan 20 1961	Nov 22 1963
Left office	Jan 20 1953	Jan 20 1961	**Nov 22 1963•**	Jan 20 1969
Birthplace	Lamar, MO	Denison, TX	Brookline, MA	Johnson City, TX
Birth date	May 8 1884	Oct 14 1890	May 29 1917	Aug 27 1908
Death date	Dec 26 1972	Mar 28 1969	Nov 22 1963	Jan 22 1973

	41. George Bush	42. Bill Clinton	43. George W. Bush	
Took office	Jan 20 1989	Jan 20 1993	Jan 20 2001	
Left office	Jan 20 1993	Jan 20 2001	—	
Birthplace	Milton, MA	Hope, AR	New Haven, CT	
Birth date	June 12 1924	Aug 19 1946	July 6 1946	
Death date	—	—	—	

29. Warren G. Harding	30. Calvin Coolidge	31. Herbert Hoover	32. Franklin D. Roosevelt
Mar 4 1921	Aug 2 1923	Mar 4 1929	Mar 4 1933
Aug 2 1923•	Mar 3 1929	Mar 3 1933	**Apr 12 1945•**
Blooming Grove, OH	Plymouth, VT	West Branch, IA	Hyde Park, NY
Nov 21 1865	July 4 1872	Aug 10 1874	Jan 30 1882
Aug 2 1923	Jan 5 1933	Oct 20 1964	Apr 12 1945

37. Richard M. Nixon	38. Gerald R. Ford	39. Jimmy Carter	40. Ronald Reagan
Jan 20 1969	Aug 9 1974	Jan 20 1977	Jan 20 1981
Aug 9 1974★	Jan 20 1977	Jan 20 1981	Jan 20 1989
Yorba Linda, CA	Omaha, NE	Plains, GA	Tampico, IL
Jan 9 1913	July 14 1913	Oct 1 1924	Feb 11 1911
Apr 22 1994	—	—	—

• Indicates the president died while in office.

★ Richard Nixon resigned before his term expired.

Index

About the Author

Don Nardo is a historian and award-winning writer who has published numerous books about American history. Among these are *The War of 1812*, *The Mexican-American War*, *The Indian Wars: From Frontier to Reservation*, *The Bill of Rights*, *The Great Depression*, and a biography of Franklin D. Roosevelt.

A longtime Jefferson enthusiast, Mr. Nardo has written extensively about various aspects of Jefferson's life and accomplishments, including his composition of the Declaration of Independence, the sources of the ideas expressed in that document, and Jefferson's feelings about and official policies regarding Native Americans. The author has included in this biography of Jefferson numerous primary (original) quotations from Jefferson himself, as well as his contemporaries. These give the text a more authentic quality, while affording the reader a glimpse into the thoughts and personal feelings of one of greatest men who ever lived.